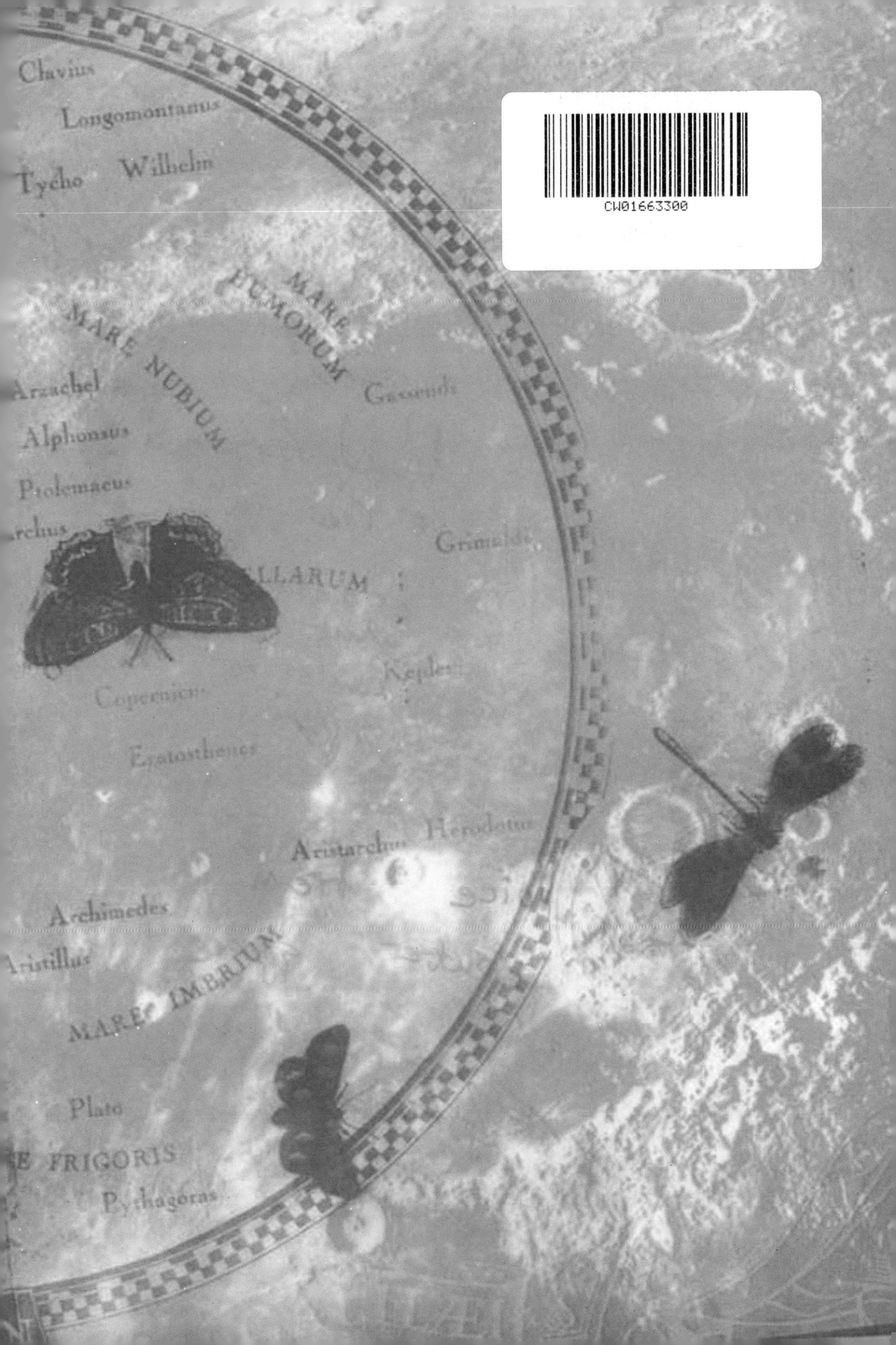
Clavius
Longomontanus
Tycho
Wilhelm
MARE HUMORUM
MARE NUBIUM
Arzachel
Alphonsus
Ptolemaeus
Gassendi
Grimaldi
Copernicus
Eratosthenes
Herodotus
Aristarchus
Archimedes
Aristillus
MARE IMBRIUM
Plato
FRIGORIS
Pythagoras

Clavius
Longomontanus
Tycho
Willhelm
MARE HUMORUM
MARE NUBIUM
Arzachel
Alphonsus
Ptolemaeus
Aristarchus
Archimedes
Aristillus
MARE IMBRIUM
Plato
FRIGORIS
Pythagoras

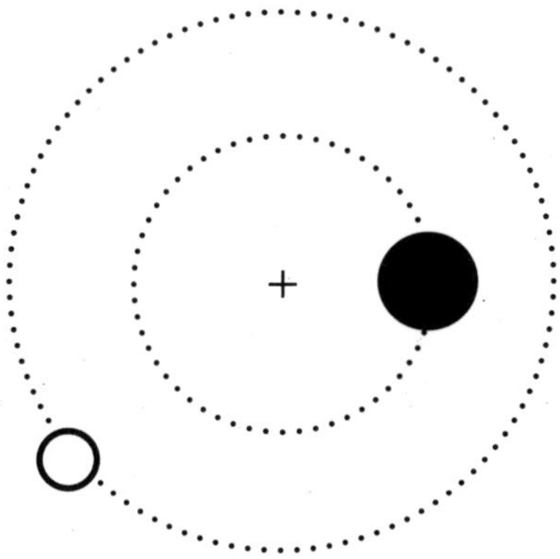

Orbiting

richard evans

illustrated by ed boxall

Aardvark Global Publishing
In Association with Moth Light Press
8 Bolebrooke Rd, Bexhill on Sea,
East Sussex, TN40 1EN

First Published in Great Britain in a limited edition of 1000 copies, 2009.

Design by Steve Burgess
steve.k.burgess@googlemail.com

Printed by Identity Press
www.identityprint.co.uk

ISBN: 978-1-4276-3759-8

But still, Moomintroll reflected on his quiet walk along the river. There are Grokes and policemen. And abysses to fall in. And it happens that people freeze to death, and blow up in the air, and fall in the sea, and catch herring-bones in their throats, and a lot of other things. The big world is dangerous.

Moominsummer Madness
Tove Jansson

Contents

–I–

—I—

O

On an ordinary beach, in view of the usual lot
of dog walkers and drowsy day-time wanderers
the sea coughs up a girl.
She claps down on the shingle.
The world folds up
and everything anyone can see is her.
Even the skidding minds of children pause on this single form
as if the sand, ice-cream and heat refuse to mingle
with what has appeared
bloated on the stones.

Then the volume is up again.
Each sound is switched in turn.
First the sea-churn, then slowly the sound
of children crying, of cars going by,
of seagulls. Then shouting
and pebbles crunching under foot
as a scatter of men clamber down the beach
not knowing what they will do
when they reach her.

Flood

I thought if I waited,
if I left wine, small purple flowers,
a polished coin, if I made secret prayers
and with rituals
blessed the dirt that would cake your boots
when you came
then you would come.

I thought if I wept,
if I fucked with the thought
of your face masking the face of the one
who has taken your place
and made of my bones
a terrible shrine
then you would come home.

And I thought if I drove
my children away, and drove
myself mad, and cut through my palm,
and bewitched the windows of your friends
with my watching –
or if I stayed numb, silent and orderly,
beached and counting the sum of your acts
with white and black pebbles, one by one,
then you would come home.

But you didn't come.

Eight stars out
and the station is calling.
Not much to eat, the clock tower is gone.
And where the river mouth was
now there's a market –
the people seem surprised
when it floods.

Prayer for the Long Walk

It is not my father's head, grey as morning embers
It is not my mother's head
It is not my brother's, nor my sister's,
Who are warm and quietly sleeping.

Only after the event do I know
The stain on my palms, the bruise on my thighs,
Only after can I smell the singed hair
From the half-plait tied to my belt-knot.

I shall wear a peacock feather with the spirit eyes
I shall wear the long earring
I shall choose the dark or light meat
Before bones are stripped and boiled.

But only after the river-long month
Eating what I dig with my nails,
Only after the mud-skin prayer
Has been sung for my foe, and myself.

It is not my father's head I take with me
It is not my mother's head
It is not my brother's, nor my sister's,
Who are warm and quietly sleeping.

Seven Steps to Understanding Death

No, you can't buy ashes on eBay
but a dead moth is a leaf with strange edges.

*

Eat steak rare. Mop up the blood.
Watch your knife part the flesh, neatly.

*

Or call the cadaver an exhibit,
her skull-cap raised in ceremonial welcome.

*

Because Bone Sliver begat Relic begat
The Vatican Seal; as red, as soft as your gums.

*

And when lines smudge, still fur and a curve of jaw,
but not a rabbit, or a jackdaw.

*

Be careful in churchyards. Don't walk on graves.
The current up your spine is future's memory.

*

With ashes, you visit a park or the sea.
When sunlight mottles your hand, you throw.

Religion

The Bible stories arrived
Stale as Noah's lost biscuit;
Blow the dust off and the words,
Dishevelled, went with it.

My mother's stories flickered
In spirited darkness. "Every
Tooth and nail numbered,
Every hair and bone."

Her favourite theme was people
Hacked up to make relics.
"But after the stigmata, it was
The single thing I wanted."

And what comes after, a heaven
For all the tiny pieces?
"Just consecrated rooms,
The utterance of secrets."

Snaggle Tooth

See her there, snaggle tooth,
face crisscrossed with cattle roads,
she's dressed like a medieval Romanian peasant
and this is Nineteen Ninety in Sussex.
She's begging for myth to colour her in,
that's plain, but the stories
spin like faces on a besmirched coin,
that lands upright, every time.
Don't listen to the fairy tales:
eleven girls in winter graves,
day by day waiting, tending their beds,
a twelfth and she will be made beautiful...
Those butterflies were cabbage whites
and are common this time of year,
the grub on her hands is street-grub
and is yours for the pittance of a month without soap.
No story grows out of pure rubbish.
Unbutton the leaves gently or the pod breaks.
Rush it, force it, and you expose sticky pulp,
not the crisp, sweet cut of velveteen skin.

–II–

In the Beginning We Played Games to Kill Time

This place is a shit stain.
Neither of us can sleep.
We play games; that's our way of sleeping.

I invented a game called 'Polypropylene Abattoir'.
You prefer to clean.
You move some rubbish, I move some rubbish,

You move some more rubbish –
It's a way of sleeping, as I said.
Shadow puppetry is out of the question.

Puns have been abolished.
I invented a game called 'Active Ingredients',
You invented a game called 'I Keep Finding Packets of
Unsmoked Cigarettes

And I Don't Smoke'.
There are too many places like this.
Only the rubbish is different, in minor details,

The same brands, but larger or smaller wrappers,
Or different plastics.
We should have a hundred words for plastic.

*

You don't like my game
'Looking through Bins for some Decent Pornography'
So I play it undercover while you're looking

Into unsealed letterboxes.
You think every letterbox should contain a poem.
You're looking for poems by Caroline Bergvall

And Marjorie Welish.
And I'm looking for pornography.
All the pornography I ever owned was printed on bark

Or grease-proof paper or dental floss or filmed
With a bamboo camera
In the time of a plague of locusts.

I invented a game called 'Why you Despise
Pornography.' But you won't play.
I've been crying a lot lately.

*

You don't call for three days.
You've been watching a sit-com about rape.
You say I'm the only person you know

That can't see the funny side of rape.
I don't know any more.
You don't want to play a game.

You want to get back to the box-set.
There are nineteen more episodes to watch,
Each named after a famous sado-masochist.

"You'd find 'Burroughs' funny. You like Burroughs."
As I said, I don't know; all the flats
Along the seafront to the brim

With ironic perverts and
Ghost tenants gouged out in mezzanines.
They set off the fire alarm eight times last week.

Club Land

Tongues mixed and mingled, horrible execration,
Shrill shreiks, hoarse groans, fierce yells and hideous blether
And clapping of hands thereto, without cessation...
— Dante, *Inferno*

A strobing of images: eyes advance
'You didn't?' Then laughter –
riotous, scouring. The mouths

theatrically wide or cupped.
Pressed to the wall or along the bar,
women, luminous thin and dressed

to show it. Each midriff, a spectre
of hunger, is assessed when passing
with pursed lips or a round of laughter.

"This is Narcissus Alley."
My poet-guide says. "They are basking,
or caught in the back-glare, weary –

are skins hooked up for the mirror."
Along the edge, as if by ritual,
or through fear of getting nearer,

humourless, prison-photo glances
from lads, pristine, with habitual
gesture arranging hair or glasses.

"Aren't they happy?" Me to my guide,
"I thought the chase is what they want."
"And so do they, it's not just pride

that keeps them stuck. Like hungry ghosts,
in all they have, they feel a lack.
A camera rolls, watching their most

thrilling times with cold rebuke:
'Is this all? Is this all you have?
Just work and sleep and drink and puke?'

So every week they end up coming
here to show themselves they're living,
but they're not. We best keep going..."

The Book of Cross Sections

Papaver rhoeas, Cantaurea cyanyus, Urtica dioica –
the hard fucks of a world before fucks.
Flipped upright and segmented
by invisible blades; capsule, stamen, stigma
in the ring of a fantasy telescope.

'Right angle to an axis.' Perfection.
Then on the seafront with a bag of soft chips,
each car that hits the net divided
into five thin strips, swivelled
vertically; here the swift knots of a carburettor,

here the ingenious viscera. In greater detail
with arrows: gears, breaks, cerebellum (of passenger).
At the next set of traffic lights, the sections
reconverge; N435 TPL resumes course.
Thirty-eight minutes a day like this,

then to the park. The Apollo bandstand
sinks, *Alnus glutinosa, Fagus sylvatica*
lurch forward, trip. A bulge of tubers
and loam lip the caesura. (Close up
and cross sections provided overleaf.)

Stop. A hand moves to a mouth, turns
and is incised in four directions. 'It gets
like a roundabout you can't stop.'
Knuckles, fibres. 'You end up forgetting
how to get off.' Fifty-one minutes

then London Road, King's Road, Warrior
Square, Number Five, Flat Five.
Stairs, key, lock. Involuntary motion.
Hall, bathroom, bathroom. Mirror;
a black and white diagram of teeth.

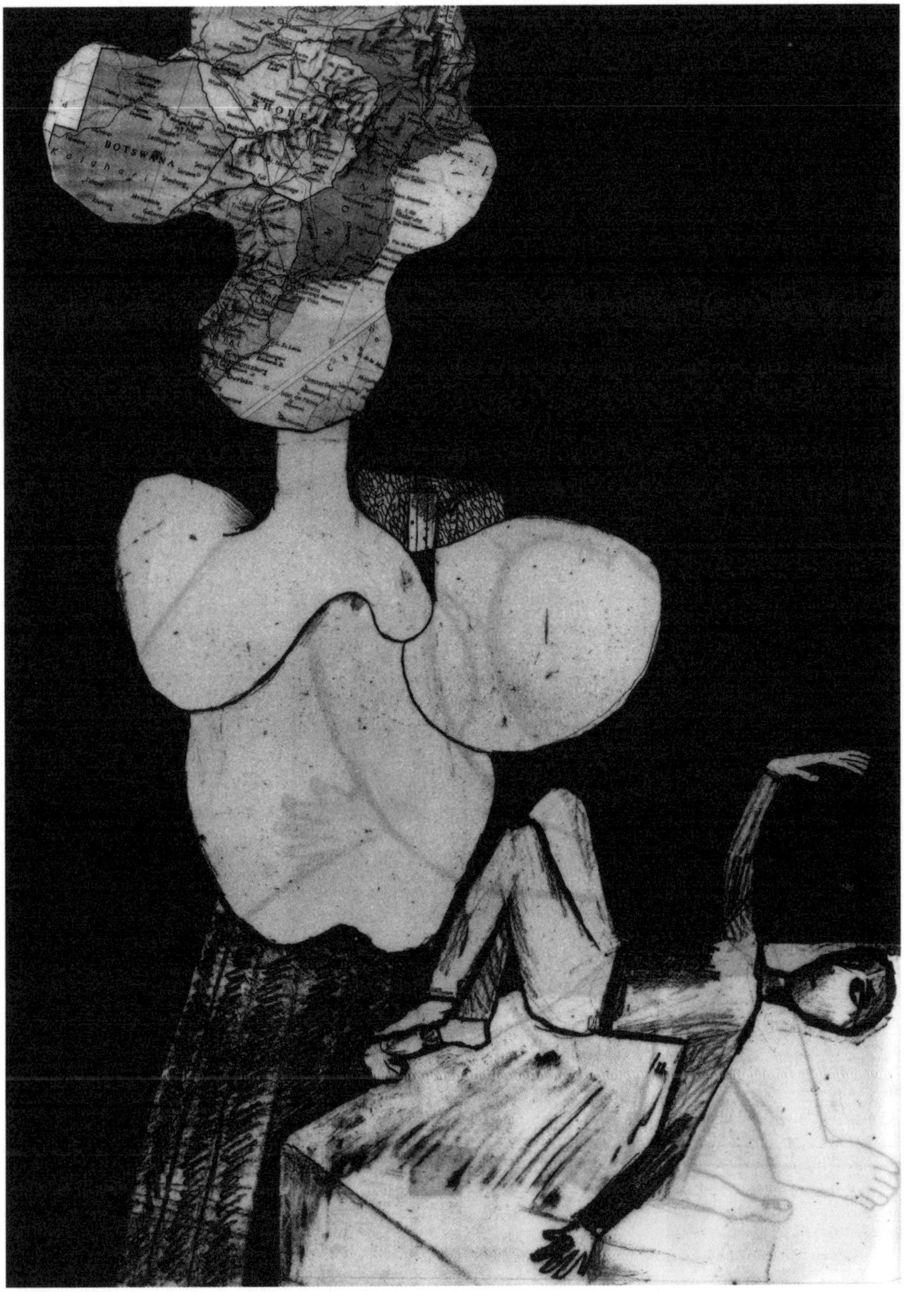
BOTSWANA

Looking for Jim

1. Camping Le Parc de la Colline, Paris

Medicine descends
through liquid night
descends, imagine
as a jelly-fish
floating down to our camp
before feeding
lithe tentacles
into ear holes up nostrils & pumping us awake

orange glow
behind shifting ferns
the woody smell and fog
break through days of snack-bar exhaustion
and we are
all at once singing
'If you believed in lizards
would you tell
the authorities?' with a midnight
chorus of crickets.

2. Boulevard de Clinchy, Montmartre

Top shelf streets
we slid timid along
harangued by lizardy men
into cupboard dusk
to wait for ancient
drapes to peel away
& show us the girls
screwing lazily at noon.

3. Père Lachaise Cemetery

The monuments of the world
are heavy bored. We place
the obligatory whiskey bottle & fags
down on the stone, stand around
with the others for a message or sign
until a face like terminal come-down
tells us to go –
and we head back heavily
through necropolis lanes,
quite away from the mad,
soft children.

O

'I thought I was in a shipping crate,
had been for years.
The sea water welled up through rust holes.
It was ceaseless ructions and breaking
and at any moment
somersaults would knock me flat.

How I had come to be there, or why
I had no conception.
I could read the story of my bruises,
the eyes of strangers, sullen,
indifferent,
and no part of me, or no part

at least of what I could remember;
the slits in metal,
the days shading dark into darker,
and in every direction the sea's vast grey
acknowledgement,
which I took to be the soul.

Had there been hope of recovery,
but there was no hope.
Though sometimes I dreamt a chisel at the latch,
a sudden dent in sea-worn armour
and a human face
leaning in... recoiling.'

-III-

Literati

A deckchair on an uncut lawn, outside
a converted train I'm staying in.
I read Keats' 'Fall of Hyperion';
a mosquito, skinless, in his high dome.

Brilliance: you learn its tug. Two horses,
mistreated, grown deranged – one bolts
to dazzlement, one, to stable dark –
each by rope tied to your trailing limbs.

Better turn to the letters at the back.
To his lover, Fanny Brawne, he writes
a wriggling squit. 'I cannot help it –
my heart seems now made of iron.' And then

a week later to a financial aid –
'the love of a woman... cloying treacle,'
and 'people are debtors for my verses.'
The ego, derailed: it makes me tired.

No doubt you remember Auden's line
on Yeats' death, 'forgiven for writing well.'
I too love the poems, but I fear the worst
when purchasing the kiss-and-tell.

Take Ezra Pound, a fascist sympathizer.
John Berryman, alcoholic womaniser.
Anne Sexton, suicide celebrator.
Philip Larkin, Thatcherite masturbator.

They pay for brilliance with their souls.
I dare to think, and am pulled up sharp –
when I watched that girl walk off a bridge,
I went home, wrote.

Encounters

Does it snow
on the moon?
ad infinitum.

That was my first poem.

It made
an atmosphere
I liked to sit in,
and stare.

Does it snow
on the moon?

Scant.

But pure
as a chant.

I said it
and snow fell
on moon craters.

Only later
a stranger came,
listened.

Does it snow on the
'No, it doesn't.'

Side Lines

Annotations are another story:
I think I'm on my own,
then scored under in pencil
I felt like a soul being prayed for.

I skim ahead for more –
find a skittish rant in biro

'He's plumped into bed
with self-delusion.' 'But that's
the point!' A third, in black,
'it's a double-bluff, a switch-back.'

Margins fill with buckled theory,
rusty on rooted axles.

And knowing all three
were one – were me – I still wonder
who wrote and why they'd bother.
Here, thickly underlined in Byron,

And then – and then – and then –

Snap

Late, this picture of Berryman, mid-flow
in Dublin. The kind of stale pub
that fits his Dream Songs;
past three hundred and still
no sniff of dregs, or sign of letting up
– what didn't go wrong?

His hand's a cage before him, set to trap
his thought and hold it. Not for sympathy,
or his mother,
but to castigate the world, the rack
they strung him to at birth; through agony
only screaming *tighter* –

And if not that, then the beard and desert holes
where his eyes should be, make a saint of him,
and prove his (much repeated) point:
even with affairs, drink, attempts and all,
though pigs may smile with their master's faces,
he was not Henry.

Between Seminars

It starts again. The body's magnets twitch
towards an undergraduate, lingering
beside you and your untouched lunch.
A field, or further skin

against which her legs lean, drawing
your metal all to one edge;
it's not just lips and scent and wetness
it's something terminal

that shunts your numerous filings loose
and turns in the ribcage
your heart like kebab meat.
Is this you? Will you always be

the bad boy from Fischl's picture?
Unobserved intruder, transfixed
by what may be stolen, but not kept:
her body outstretched in slatted light.

What I Have

Your friend sobs on the phone again
holds the line up for hours with the sound
of churned traffic and distant radio.
In our borrowed flat we live like seashells
at the bottom of a cupboard.

But I have something for you, sprung
silver flapping from my mouth –
I've wrapped it up here. I've been meaning
to lay it in your lap, to let you feel its mass.
I've been meaning to lay it by your ear while you sleep.

But there hasn't been time somehow,
or somehow I pulled it apart.
I found airy fragments all over.
In lonely motorway garages.
In pub toilets. Peering out
From the inside of balloons.

And now I have it all at once and hold it out to you
I see it is nothing special after all,
not the fish glint and swerve I had hoped for –
but a leaf in a winter letterbox
with no words on it.

Love Song
For Sally

I can force my way out of bed
I can come to see you, your rainy roof.
I can press my eyes open,
the loud dream that tornadoes
around here, shut out for the afternoon.
And I can speak like a flute.
I can hang your breath on the gnats
sewing up a tiny piece of the sky.
Or I can cry, a little, to loosen the clay
from your lashes, all this because I love you
in the way poor, sleepy things love.

Inside my body there are marching men
bruising the earth with their boots.
I cannot reveal the things they chant
as the sea can pull back
and show off its earnings –
but I can press, tenderly,
a star-blemish through eyelids,
with my lips I can tease out a galaxy.

–IV–

Orbiting

Say a radio broadcast was sent
the wrong way and circled the moon,
breaking waves after ninety years orbit
with the stern, plum English of the dead.

Say we unearthed her diary.

Though not many heard, only those tuning
at that precise moment, fuzz interrupted
by curious diction; while beginning to thaw
in the warmth of the breath, a clasp of ice

delicately snapping –

Dear Synapse

I swing a sudden left off the main road
into nervy light, and I'm out,
hurtling towards an anonymous town.
I could be speeding down branches
in a shattered quartz, the moment's sky
is cinematic – the asphalt, brilliant white.

Once anything set memory sparking.
Bad handwriting, a word in a book.
I'd find her trailing a rail-track
through woods, almost real, still
in her grey Converse – inching
a shadow along the rail.
We'd sit and talk for a while.

Today it's just a skin I find
on musselled rock, the furthest out.
I follow down an unmarked path,
down steps almost reclaimed by marl,
to where it's caught, intact. It could be lint,
or diaphanous seaweed, if not
for the translucent print, the watermark.

Goose Egg

In 1233, in Mainz, Conrad Torso of Marburg, emissary to the Pope, condemned a young widow to imprisonment in a goose egg.

Possession of lime snakes
and the seven enchantments,
possession of birth-stones.

A sideways gait,
a cuprous tongue.

Possession of indices,
possession of birth-charts.

Counting the dead on her fingers in Rhineland.
Tuning violas in Mainz
to the diabolical scale.

The six indications
and the burns –
shiny, puckered like mouths of carp.

To be buried
beneath mounds of hair
until spirit loosens;

To be drawn
by incantations
into albumen.

Pietà

Jesus I climbed up on your knee
when the Biggest Club in Middle Europe closed
to attend the lines in your beard. Remember?

It is your consciousness, that no one can hack into;
not hairs depicted but synapses – not a nose,
but the extensive neuronal assembly expected

of someone like you. Charles Bridge
was hugging up against us, morning cleared.
Your mother looked straight through me.

Recall? My finger pressing your lip?
The words of a single song? I sang every song I know.

When Miracles Happen

Jeremiah in the liver-spots of a dock leaf.
Isaiah in the flex of a saw.
Crumbs patterned on the chopping board.

When you're small, there's a tableau
through a spy-hole; fairy lights
where his crown should be, the body of Christ packed in

with children's books and the Christmas tree.
You get big, imagine that's over,
then a wave swipes your shoe with a beard

the same fortnight two priests,
one Northern, one Welsh, leave message
after message on your answerphone.

It's the joke life plays when the wrong thought
is better, to say martyr when you mean
to say mother,

Saviour, when you only mean father.
Repeat with me now until it rhymes with your breath
a dock leaf is a dock leaf is a dock leaf

Love Letter to Tove Jansson

So long since I've seen you
through the milk glass of morning
on your way to the cliff top.
Once we agreed, every morning
to meet as light broke on the ridge
overlooking the tin house
where your mother and sister
are curled up soft. I've overslept:
a sad sleep has moored me
among wind-up toys and flowers
made of cloth – until this morning.
Now across the blanket marsh
I am coming, with handfuls of peonies
and a slow song on my lips, fully formed,
one part expectation,
two parts spring sadness
and for the rest just the colossal
delight of being alone.

Clavius
Longomontanus
Tycho
Wilhelm
MARE HUMORUM
MARE NUBIUM
Arzachel
Alphonsus
Ptolemaeus
Kepler
Copernicus
Eratosthenes
Aristarchus
Herodotus
Archimedes
Aristillus
MARE IMBRIUM
Plato
FRIGORIS
Pythagoras

Clavius
Longomontanus
Tycho
Wilhelm
MARE HUMORUM
MARE NUBIUM
Arzachel
Gassendi
Alphonsus
Ptolemaeus
Grimaldi
Kepler
Copernicus
Eratosthenes
Herodotus
Aristarchus
Archimedes
MARE IMBRIUM
Plato
FRIGORIS
Pythagoras